The World's
Weirdest Looking Animals
ISBN- 9781960612786

Gobi Jerboa have big ears, and excellent hearing. They are nocturnal and see great in the dark. They get around by jumping just like a rabbit. They can leap 9 feet. They don't drink water. They get all the water they need from what they eat.

The streaked tenrec is the only mammal species practicing stridulation. This is when an animal rubs together parts of its body to give out a sound. This technique is more common for insects and snakes. Tenrecs are nocturnal and quite shy. Just the shape and color of the tenrec catches your eye. It has quills like a porcupine and is brightly colored with yellow.

The naked mole rat has no fur. Unlike most other mammals, they cannot maintain a steady body temperature because they have no fur. They live in large groups called a colony and huddle to stay warm. Naked mole rats are capable of living over 30 years, unlike most rats that only live a few years.

Star Nosed Mole. Each one of the 22 tentacle-like projections contain numerous highly sensitive organs, which help to identify potential food items. Star nosed Moles are excellent swimmers and have even been seen swimming under ice. Their nose isn't used for smelling, it's used for touch to feel around, and find food in darkness.

Echidna, along with the platypus, the echidna is the only other living egg laying mammal species. They have the second lowest body temperature after the platypus. Which is good news for their life span. They've been known to live for up to 50 years. They might look fearsome because of their spiny exterior, but these animals are shy. When confronted or frightened, they will curl up into a ball, tucking in its snout and legs. Hiding and protecting themselves with an armor of spikes.

Binturongs have extremely long tails which they use to balance when moving along tree limbs. They are often described as smelling like buttered popcorn because their urine contains a chemical compound that gives popcorn its aroma.

Patagonian mara looks like a cross between a rabbit and a kangaroo. They bounce or hop like rabbits. They can jump 7 feet in one hop. They are the world's fastest rodent. They can run 30 miles per hour. Be careful when approaching one. They can spray their urine at you.

They are nervous animals, and very bouncy. They don't make good pets.

Saiga antelope. Take a look at its nose. It has long fat bulging nostrils. Their nose because of its size, helps it to breathe freely in the dusty desert conditions. The secret is that their nose is lined with hair inside, which filters the dust out of the air. They also use their nose to produce loud sounds almost like elephants. It can stretch its nose out to make different sounds.

Markhors have long twisty horns that can grow up 5 feet long. They are the largest of all the wild goat species. Males can grow to well over 200 pounds. They are extremely skilled climbers. These goats can even climb trees and other slanted structures, including dangerous cliffs. The hooves of the markhor are wide, helping them to balance when climbing on uneven surfaces. This helps them, so they do not fall off the mountains slopes.

Okapis belong to the Giraffe family. But are related to the zebra. That's why they have partial zebra stripes. They can stand on their back feet to eat leaves off trees. That's how they got the nickname of TreeHugger.

Wild Okapis only live in the regions of Congo jungle.

The male Tufted deer has long teeth that look like fangs. The fangs can grow up to two inches long. Tufted deer are named for the black tuft of hair on their head. They don't have big antlers like other deer. So, they use their fangs to help protect them.

The babirusa pig looks weird because it has multiple tusks that grow in any direction. These tusks are elongated canine teeth that grow upwards from the upper jaw and curve towards the forehead. The babirusa has been called a wild pig with a dental problem. They are found in the forests of Southeast Asia. Despite their heavy wait and size, they are good swimmers.

The tapir's long snout isn't just for looks. It's prehensile, meaning it's made to wrap around and grab things. Tapirs use their noses to grab fruit, leaves, and other food. They can eat 75 pounds of food per day. Their Closest Relatives Are Rhinos and Horses

Warthogs are an odd-looking animal. The large tusks of a warthog are enlarged canine teeth. They have two pairs. They are named for the wart on the sides of their face. However, these are not warts, but rather protrusions made up of bone and cartilage. Warthogs can survive long periods of time without water. They are fast and can run up to 30 miles per hour.

The dik-dik is a very small antelope. It only grows about 15 inches high. They only weigh about 13 pounds. Most dogs way more than a dik-dik does. When dik-diks feel they're in danger, they hide instead of fleeing from predators. When frightened or disturbed, they make a whistling sound through their nose that sounds like "zik-zik," and this is probably how they got their name.

Gerenuk Deer has a long narrow neck. The gerenuk eats standing on two legs. They stand erect on their hind legs, with their long necks extended, to browse on tall bushes. By using their front legs to pull down higher branches, they can reach leaves six to eight feet off the ground.

Under all that fur there is a rabbit. Angora rabbits have super soft and long fur, making them look like big and cuddly fluff balls. Angora rabbits are the oldest type of domestic rabbit. Angoras require lots of grooming. They are active and playful. They enjoy the company of cats, and always enjoy companionship with their owners and other rabbits.

The Komondor dog is known for its unique coat. It has a double coat. With a dense, soft, woolly undercoat and an overcoat made up of strong, tassel-like cords that form naturally from coarse, wavy, or curly hair. The cords, which feel like felt, grow longer with age. Maintaining their coat requires a lot of work. They are very smart. They are a type of herding dog for sheep and other animals.

Peterbald cats can either be hairless or have short fur. As you notice they have big ears. Despite their appearance, Peterbald's are friendly, sweet-tempered, and incredibly rare cats. They make loyal pets and form deep attachments to their owners. Peterbald's are one of the newest cat breeds. Peterbald cats are exceptionally outgoing and energetic.

The Sphynx and the elf cat are related. They are both hairless cats. These cats are mainly indoor cats. They can't handle cooler temperatures because they have no fur. If left outside they can get sunburn or freeze easily. They hate being alone and enjoy the company of people and other pets. They are incredibly sociable, playful, and intelligent.

The Oriental Shorthair is thought to be one of the most intelligent cat breeds, if not the most intelligent. They are highly trainable because they are very curious and love interaction and stimulation. They get very attached to people, very quickly. Oriental Shorthairs love to bond with their family. They are agile and athletic and known as highly skilled jumpers.

Levkoy cats are kid friendly, and they easily bond with every member of the family. They are often friendly toward strangers, serving as marvelous ambassadors. They are highly inquisitive, with an uncanny ability to open cupboards and drawers. Their ears lay flatter than most cats. They can be hairless or have hair.

The Fossa cat is not a pet. It is a wild cat. Their face has different features, and they don't look like a true cat. The fossa is one of the top predators on the island of Madagascar. Fossa's have scent glands that release a stinky smell when the animal is irritated or frightened. Fossa cats are expert climbers and like to live in trees. They have no fur on the bottom of their feet, which allows them to grip trees easier with their claws.

Aye-ayes can be found only in the forests of Madagascar. It looks like a cross between a raccoon and a rat. The animal rarely descends from its treetop home to the forest floor. Only active at night, they spend the day snoozing on branches in nests made of leaves. Big, yellow eyes let it see in the dark. Giant, sensitive ears help the animal detect bugs and other critters to eat.

The Sunda colugo lives in trees. It has skin attached to its underbody. They will jump from a tree and spread open their legs.

When they spread open their legs, the skin on their underbody spreads out, and allows them to glide through the air.

The Honduran white bat has a yellow horn on its nose. Bats usually don't have horns like a rhino. They are also completely white except for their feet, legs, ears, and horn are yellow. Most bats are brown to black in color. It's a really tiny bat that will fit in between your fingers.

The marabou stork has been dubbed the undertaker bird because of its appearance. When seen from behind, the marabou stork's back and wings appear cloak-like.

The marabou stork is lazy and spends most of its time standing around. The marabou stork is a huge bird that cannot be mistaken for anything else when spotted.

The Kakapo is a large green parrot with a distinctive owl-like face, and they waddle like a duck when they walk. The Kakapo is the only parrot that cannot fly, but they climb trees well. They are one of the longest-lived bird species in the world, estimated to live to 90 years old. They are green in color.

Sri Lanka Frogmouth is named because its mouth looks like a frog's mouth. This frogmouth is rarely seen during the day except at roost sites or when flushed. To hide, they lift their head straight back and remain perfectly still.

The Potoo has large yellow eyes. They have very thin eyelids and can see you even with their eyes closed. Great Potoos are shy. They spend most of their time hidden away in tall tree branches. They are solitary creatures who don't even live in groups with others. To hide, they just close their eyes and remain motionless.

Frigatebirds have a red bladder or waddle that they can puff up. Even though frigatebirds are seabirds, their feathers aren't waterproof, so they can't land in the ocean. Frigatebirds have long, thin, hooked beak that is specially designed to help them catch slippery fish.

The Philippine eagle has a head crest that makes it look majestic. The Philippine Eagle was named the national bird of the Philippines in 1995. The Philippine Eagle is one of the rarest birds in the world. It is considered the largest of the extant eagles in the world in terms of length and wing surface area.

The Shoebill stork gets its name from its beak, which looks like a pair of old-style clog shoes. The shoebill stork looks like a prehistoric animal. Shoebill storks have a habit of shaking their heads back and forth and they chatter their beaks together as a type of communication.

The Lyrebird has long tail feathers that it can extend forward over its head. The lyrebird has powerful legs with long toes and claws, which they use for raking through dead leaves and soil to find their food. They can also mimic other sounds.

The Long-Wattled Umbrellabird has a wattle on its throat that can grow over 13 inches long. It also has long crest feathers that makes it look like it has a rounded head. They are not very good flyers, they look clumsy when flying.

The superb bird of paradise. This is what it looks like normally. Below is a picture of what it looks like when it spreads out its feathers.

It spreads out its feathers to make itself look bigger as a defense mechanism to scare off other animals.

The Silkie Chicken is very fluffy. Yup under all those feathers, there is a chicken. It's amazing they can even see through all those feathers. Silkie chickens are friendly birds and easy to hand raise. They make good pets. Some owners groom them and spend time enjoying their companionship. They get their name because their feathers feel like silk.

Cassowaries are the third tallest bird in the world, they can grow to six feet tall. They have a crown on their head. They also have large feet with very sharp claws. They have strong legs and can run 31 miles per hour and jump 7 ft straight in the air. One last cool fun fact is they lay green eggs.

The Royal Flycatchers most notable feature is their fan-shaped crest, which folds down when unused. They communicate with each other by using slow, plaintive moves and whistles. Some research suggests their crests may startle or scare away other birds and animals. They also use it to attract insect that they will eat.

The paradise tanager is a tropical bird with feathers in blue, red, light green, and black. Paradise tanagers are hard to spot, because they like to be at the highest part of a tree. Their colors have inspired many artists and their images have been used on postage stamps around the world.

Wilson's bird of paradise has a blue head cap with red and yellow colors and circular tail feathers. Very cool looking bird. It makes one of the noisiest calls of all birds. It sounds like a car alarm going off and can be heard from a long distance.

The Platypus has a long bill that looks like an elongated duck's bill. They might look cute and cuddly. But the male platypus is venomous. They have a hollow spur on each hind leg connected to a venom secreting gland, and their venom can be lethal.

The Pink fairy armadillo. Found only in central Argentina, this is the smallest armadillo species in the world. Like other armadillos, pink fairy armadillos have a shell but it's softer, thinner and more flexible and covers about half their body. The shell's pink color comes from all the blood vessels close to its surface. Giving it a pink color.

Pangolin means roller. When a Pangolin is in danger, it will roll up into a ball and can be rolled around. They have a hard shell that also protects them. There are eight species of pangolin, and they are built like an armadillo. They have sharp front claws for digging.

The Aardvark. The name aardvark is an African word which literally means earth pig. They have a long snout and huge ears. The tongue of an aardvark can reach up to 12 inches in length. Which helps them to grab ants and termites, their main food source. They have very sharp claws to help them dig up their favorite food.

The Anteater is just a weird looking animal. With long legs and a long snout used for scooping up ants and termites, its favorite food. An anteater's tongue is 2 feet long and can flick in and out of its mouth 150 times per minute to grab ants. Their tongue has sticky saliva and spines on it to help grab the ants and termites. They can eat up to 30,000 ants and termites each day.

The Sloth got its name because it moves really slow. Everything is sluggish and slow moving, even food digestion. They are faster in the water than they are on land. They spend most of their lives hanging in the trees. They have bad eyesight and can hardly see at all.

White faced saki monkeys are black except for their white face. White faced saki are dramatic when they feel threatened. They fluff up and vigorously shake their body hair, then stomp their feet in an arched-back posture.

The tarsier monkey has huge eyes that look almost alien like. Tarsiers are some of the oldest primates on the planet, dating back at least 55 million years. Tarsiers are the only carnivorous primates. They eat insects, lizards, and snakes. They are one of the smallest monkeys on the planet.

The gelada monkey looks like it's wearing a cape. Its fur is thin on the chest and neck, exposing its skin. They are shuffle feeders who rarely stand up when grazing. They prefer to continuously pluck grass blades while shuffling from place to place on their bottoms. They use a mix of facial expression and vocalizations to communicate with others in the group. Just like humans do.

The emperor tamarin monkey has a long mustache. It is believed that they were named after German emperors who also wore a mustache. Emperor tamarins live in groups of two to as many as 15 monkeys. Emperor Tamarins are very small, normally weighing around one pound. These tiny primates are playful and friendly.

De Brazza's monkeys store food in their cheek pouches while they forage, then eat it later when they are in a safe place. Just like chipmunks do. It is one of the most widespread African primates. It can be differentiated from other monkeys by its orange crest on its head and white beard. They are extremely territorial and its better off not to approach them. They do not like to be around humans.

The red shanked douc monkey has some weird features. It looks like it's wearing a hat on its head. Its legs are red and looks like it's wearing a pair of stockings. Which run from its knees to its ankles. That's how it got its name. They like to eat leaves. They have several sacs in their stomach filled with bacteria that breaks down the leaves it eats. Which bloats them up and gives them a pot belly.

The gee's golden langur monkey has face features that resemble a person. They got their name from their gold colored fur. They are social and generally live in troops of up to 50 monkeys. This monkey works hard to avoid humans. Making them extremely difficult to observe in the wild.

Lorises monkeys often hang upside down from branches by their feet so they can use both hands to eat. They sleep curled up in a ball with their head between their knees and their legs hooked over their head. Their large eyes give them phenomenal vision, even in dim light or darkness of the forest.

The Snub Nose Monkey got its name from its very small or flat nose. The golden snub nose monkey has a blue mask around its eyes. Snub nosed monkeys are highly social. They form large troops or groups in the summer of as many as 600 individuals. Snub nosed monkeys spend the majority of their life living in the trees.

The owl monkey got its name because of its large eyes that resemble an owl's eyes. They are completely nocturnal, and their eyes help them to see at night. They are also called the night monkey because they only come out when its dark. The owl monkey has a heavily furred body and tail and is characterized by its large eyes and round head.

The Patas monkey has a unique looking mustache. Patas monkeys spend most of their time on the ground rather than in trees. Patas monkeys are the fastest primates on Earth. They can run 34 miles per hour. They can walk and run on their hind feet. Patas monkeys communicate through visual cues rather than vocalizations.

The Bald uakari has a red face and ears. It almost looks like it has bad sunburn. They are intelligent and peaceful. They are social and like to live in large troops or groups. Their tails are the shortest of all monkeys. Bald uakaris wave their tails when excited, just like dogs do. Living in flooded forests, it's no surprise that uakaris can swim relatively well. They can make at least 10 different types of facial expressions.

The Proboscis monkey got its name because of its nose long and puffed nose. Proboscis monkeys are great swimmers. They've have webbed feet and hands to help them to swim. As well as being agile in trees, the proboscis monkey has been known to leap into the water from heights. The proboscis monkey is also known as the long-nosed monkey.

Author Page

Billy Grinslott & Kinsey Marie Books

ISBN – 9781960612786

Thanks

www.ingramcontent.com/pod-product-compliance
Lightning Source LLC
Chambersburg PA
CBHW060822270326
41931CB00002B/55